AF256461

THE MARKETING FALLACY

NORGRESS BOOKS

An Imprint by Norgress
books.norgress.com

Copyright © 2020 Joshua Littlejohn.

All rights reserved.

Thank you for purchasing an authorized copy of this book. Your purchase helps to support writers, editors, narrators, typesetters, and designers. In complying with copyright laws, we ask that you do not copy, scan, or redistribute any part of this book.

Norgress Books and the mountain colophon are trademarks of Norgress.

Published in Canada.

Paperback ISBN: 978-1-7773310-0-9
eBook ISBN: 978-1-7773310-1-6
Audiobook ISBN: 978-1-7773310-2-3

FIRST EDITION

THE MARKETING FALLACY

How Any Small Business Can
Look Like A Large Corporation,
Without The Large Costs

JOSHUA LITTLEJOHN
with STANLEY GATERO

Though the author has made every effort to supply the most accurate and up-to-date mentions, web addresses, and contact details at the time of this publication, both the author and publisher cannot assume any responsibility for errors or changes that may have occurred after publishing.

No responsibility is assumed for any third parties mentioned.

DEDICATION

To small business owners, like my father.
You all work relentlessly and sacrifice so much to
pursue your dreams while providing for the ones
you love. You are legends. Thank you.

CONTENTS

INTRODUCTION

There are numerous misconceptions about marketing. These range from "marketing is for the big dogs" to "it is too time-consuming". These misconceptions are what I like to refer to as "marketing fallacies". They are the excuses that many small businesses give to justify their limited expansion efforts, plateau earnings and minimize their client base. These fallacies are what prevent several small businesses from becoming household names. Instead, they are reduced to being local favorites.

Now don't get me wrong, there is absolutely nothing wrong with being a popular local business. But, with the rise of globalization and large corporations stepping in to take hold of smaller business markets, small businesses will need to adapt quickly if they want to remain.

Need proof of this? We need not look any further than Uber's impact on local taxi businesses. Or Amazon's effect on local bookstore sales – I mean, you probably bought this book from Amazon, right? The fact is, these are only two examples of how large conglomerates can step in at any moment and quell once-thriving community sectors. These industry giants presented consumers with an alternative they couldn't resist and successfully stole the market's attention. For any business that has mastered their product or service, their funding, teams and procedures, the last piece of the business puzzle is marketing. Many small businesses have managed to conquer those initial factors already. While they might not have mastered them on the scale of Amazon or Uber, they have mastered them nonetheless. This is where marketing comes into play. Marketing for a small business can be the gateway to capturing the attention of millions – and in the digital age, it is now easier than ever.

In **The Marketing Fallacy**, I'll discuss how small businesses can overcome some of the most common misconceptions surrounding marketing, including the most misleading of them; marketing is too expensive. This might have been true a few decades ago but now, the internet has created a platform that anyone can step on and showcase themselves to the world. Just ask the thousands of YouTube stars and Instagram influencers who seemingly call the internet home.

Despite doing my degree in marketing, and intensely studying the field for the past five years, I've found that most of my knowledge came from my hands-on experience with starting my company, Norgress, and working with numerous other businesses.

Norgress is a digital media and information

technology company that started in 2017 using a $500 withdrawal from my savings account. In less than four years, I've been more than fortunate to work with numerous ventures – from young startups to established multinationals. The structure I've established at my company has frequently made others think of it as far larger than it is.

That $500 investment has turned into tens of thousands in personal income, helped me commission teams from around the world and craft an impressive client base, all while earning high-value professional connections and before graduating college. I can't chalk that up to luck. Instead, it has been the result of much trial. Norgress is the outcome of a deliberate effort to grab the attention of target audiences by positioning a small player so that it is perceived as a much larger one.

This book will provide you with the same

resources that I used to direct attention to my company. I'll share with you the low-cost tools and strategies that I've used to grow my company, and also to help other businesses fashion themselves like a market leader and showcase to the world all they have to offer. This book is about giving your market the opportunity to see what exactly makes your business so great. After reading this book, you'll know what to do to position any startup to look like a megacorp. You'll be on your way to building brand recognition in your industry, attracting new clients, and increasing your earnings.

PART 1

BUILDING THE FOUNDATION

Some quotes seem like they've earned a permanent place in daily vocabulary, like the Maya Angelou quote, "When someone shows you who they are, believe them the first time". The same can be said about the quote, "You only have one chance to make a good first impression". These clichés are clichés for a reason. They hold some truth.

Maya's statement referred to people who are close to us. Because of our mental and emotional connections, we frequently don't see them for who they are. Instead, we try to convince ourselves that they are somehow different, somehow better than they are. The fact is, in business-to-consumer relations, this well-liked quote has no place. Consumers see your company for what it is from day one and trying to change that consensus is like trying to touch your nose with your tongue; it's almost impossible to do. For that reason, I suggest that businesses adhere to the second quote and remember that they only have one chance to make an excellent first impression. An excellent first impression starts with laying a solid foundation.

One mistake a lot of small businesses make is not establishing their brand from the get-go. Consequently, whenever they earn the attention of their audience, there is nothing for them to stand on, and that attention is short-lived. What I have noticed is once you've had an audience's attention and lose it, it's challenging to regain it. So, before drawing attention to your venture, make sure you are ready for it.

·········

Work While Your Brand Is Still Unknown

Amy Renee Noonan was a part of the pop duo Karmin

American singer and songwriter, **Amy Renee Noonan**, was one half of the viral 2010's pop duo, Karmin. As part of the group, she released three

Billboard top 100 studio albums and a few platinum singles like *Brokenhearted* and *Acapella*. Following the dissolution of the group in 2017, Amy began her solo career under the stage name Qveen Herby. In a 2020 interview with music YouTuber Honest, when asked about going viral, Herby indicated that going viral is a blessing *IF* you have built your brand first.

"Every day that you're not popped off yet is a blessing that you should take advantage of."

She stated that one major factor to her group's success was that they had already created a brand for themselves, including dozens of songs, videos, social media posts, and photoshoots. She expressed that once audiences discovered them, they could binge on their past works and learn more about the group. Herby affirmed that other artists should do the same thing. As for me, I'd affirm that businesses do this.

You don't want to gain attention with no way of

keeping it.

I have never met an entrepreneur who didn't think their idea would be the next big thing or that their company didn't have the potential to be a shoo-in for market acceptance. Not achieving this often leaves them asking, "Why haven't I had my big break yet?" Well, if you are among the countless entrepreneurs asking that question, you're in a fortunate position. It might not be obvious, but this time is a godsend. Use it wisely.

In this chapter, we'll explore the steps needed to construct a solid business foundation, so that once your company's big break comes, you'll be ready. You would have already created a structure that retains the market's attention and solidifies their interest in you. It won't be easy, and there will be errors, but that is the point of doing this before you catch your audience's attention. It's far better to make your mistakes when no one is watching.

By the end of this chapter, you will be well on your way to constructing a brand that looks far larger than the real size of your company. It will be a brand that you are proud to showcase and one that will retain the attention of your audience.

DESIGNING AN IMPACTFUL LOGO

If you want to be taken seriously, then you're going to need a serious look; and by serious, I mean professional. This is where your logo comes into play. Your logo will be the face of your company, and much like faces in real life, it's the attractive ones that get the attention. But before we can begin work on your company's new face, we first need to decide how that face will look.

The best logos are those that capture their company's tone, mood and feel. They make a statement without being too loud, and a great logo will even tell a story. Let's examine some logos that do this successfully.

FedEx Corporation

If you look carefully between the "E" and "X" of the FedEx logo, you might notice something a little interesting; an arrow. Its inclusion was by no means a coincidence. According to the logo's designer, Lindon Leader, "The arrow connotes forward direction, speed and precision, and if it remained hidden, there might be an element of surprise – that aha moment."

Amazon.com, Inc.

Perhaps the most recognizable logo in the e-commerce industry, Amazon has a little-known intricacy in its logo design that adds to its iconic recognition. The logo's smile starts at the "A" of Amazon and ends at the "Z", intentionally. It indicates the company's stocking of goods from A to Z. Reportedly, the company's founder had a massive contribution to the logo design. Jeff Bezos was said to have attended all logo related meetings where he authorized the whole thing himself.

Apple Inc.

Apple's logo wasn't always the simplistic and literal logo that we know today. The company's first logo, designed in 1976, looked like a middle ages coat of arms. The logo was created by Ronald Wayne and it featured Isaac Newton framed in a shield and wrapped with ribbons reading "Apple Computer Co." It was made to showcase that an apple inspired something as great as the law of gravity.

Apple's first logo was used in 1976.

Points gained for storytelling through a logo. But whatever points Apple earned were lost in the logo's execution. It was too much, too literal. The following year, the logo was replaced with the bitten apple that we have come to know. Apple's current logo references its original story while being simple, memorable, and easier to reproduce.

MARKETING ACTIVITY

The Stories Behind The Brands

Get out a piece of paper, think of five companies that are widely respected or memorable, and write them down. Your list might include companies such as NIKE, Disney, Starbucks, BMW, or Twitter. Regardless of who you choose, once you have created your list, start researching each company. Is there a story behind the brand? What is that story? Can you identify it within their logo?

After completing the *Stories Behind The Brands* activity, you will have noticed a common thread. The most memorable brands of our time all seem to start with a story. So, I encourage you to also start with a story. The best place to showcase that story isn't in a paragraph on your About Us page. Instead, tell that story through the part of your company that people will see the most; your logo. A great story fuels a great brand. It's your pitch. It's what you can use to say, "This is why we matter."

For me, my company's story started with its name. "Norgress" is the combination of two words "northern" and "progress". The word "northern" represents the company's roots; being a Canadian-based startup was an emblem of pride. The second word, "progress," referred to the company's goal to help other businesses progress in their respective industries. So, I got to thinking, "What would be mostly symbolic of that?" After much brainstorming, I pictured a mountain. A mountain, in my opinion, was symbolic of stability and an upward outlook.

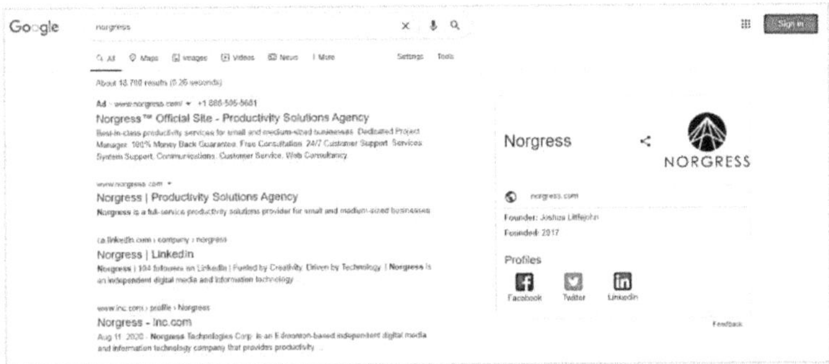

The Norgress logo as featured in Google search results.

I also asked myself, "What do I ultimately want my company to represent?" For your business, you must do the same. You might ask yourself:

- **Why did I start my business?**
- **Who is my business targeting?**
- **How will my business help them?**

Now, when crafting your logo, see how best you can infuse the answers to those questions. Just try not to be too literal, or you'll end up with another 1976 Apple logo on your hands. Instead, aim for subtle inclusions, that when discovered, induce an *ah-ha* from your audience, much like FedEx's hidden arrow.

If done correctly, whenever your audience sees your company's logo, they will also subconsciously see that story. Make sure to communicate this story to your graphic designer, and like Amazon's Bezos, be involved in the design process. Too many founders simply delegate this vital task. Often, the result is a meaningless, generic, and forgettable image that will now have to serve as the face of their company.

Once you have a logo, you'll be using it for years to come. After all, it's through constant use of that logo that you'll build brand recognition.

Don't Be That Guy

"My favorite color is _______, so I think I should go with that color for my logo."

I can't tell you how many times I've heard entrepreneurs use a phrase like that.

Whatever you do, please do not create a logo with color as its starting point. Sure, some colors will have specific mental associations, but if you genuinely want a logo that will stand the test of time and be cemented in the hearts and minds of your audience, craft your logo based on a story instead.

GETTING A PROFESSIONAL WEBSITE

An online property is a place on the web that your company occupies. They serve as the foundation of your online brand. These are the places where your audience can and will find you and connect with you. My first advice to any entrepreneur is to build a solid online property. The best online property is a website. Your company's website is its home on the internet. Despite all the many social media platforms, a website has always been my number one recommendation to all the small business owners I've worked with. Why? Well, although social media is undoubtedly a great tool, the reality is, those platforms simply aren't yours, at least not entirely. You'll be playing by their rules and their policies, and abiding by their terms.

·········

Your Website Is Your Headquarters

Barbara Corcoran featured in a Corcaran.com Billboard.

Real estate mogul **Barbara Corcoran** was among the very first realtors to establish an online property in the form of a website. The website went live in 1996 under the *Corcoran.com* domain name. There, Corcoran and her team posted available properties, open house events, and an industry-first: video walkthroughs of properties. After posting the videos, the company sold two New York apartments, sight unseen, to buyers in Japan. Corcoran's new home on the internet helped catapult them from 19th to 4th place in their market. Before the launch of their website, the Corcoran Company relied on posting classified ads in the newspaper and word-of-mouth marketing, consequently limiting their reach to the New York area. Although they still used newspaper advertising and word-of-mouth marketing to attract visitors to their new website, the website gave them unique access to other national and international markets. It allowed them to utilize far more marketing resources than any newspaper commercial could offer. The company's website is frequently credited with influencing other realtors to use the digital space.

Fast forward to today, and *Corcoran.com* is still one of the top real estate websites in the world, with an estimated 1.2 million monthly visitors, according to data from SimilarWeb.

A website is still one of the best marketing tools there is. It gives you complete autonomy because the entrepreneur has full control over their site's functionality, the look and the feel.

Websites are always changing. The ones that looked good yesterday don't look good today. One of the most challenging tasks an entrepreneur will face is constructing their website so that it is highly functional, innovative and contemporary without blowing their budget. In my case, I was fortunate enough to have some technical knowledge and skills in web development. I built my website, *Norgress.com*, myself, and got the help of a few freelancers along the way. If you have the necessary technical skills and the time, there are plenty of great website builders, courses and tutorials online that you can use to create a stunning website on your own.

These include the famous WordPress, Squarespace and Weebly, and for those with high technical knowledge, there is also Webflow. However, the fact of the matter is that most small business owners either don't have these skills, or they just don't have the time to invest. So how do you get a website that commands attention and respect without breaking the bank or learning coding in your spare time?

Most successful entrepreneurs will tell you that one of the essential skills that any entrepreneur can have is the ability to *hire* the right people. Over the years, through hiring countless contractors and freelancers, I have come to observe a few factors that have given me the edge in any negotiation.

Here are my tips to help with finding the best web designers at the best price:

1. Understand the job (and the industry)

Take a few hours to educate yourself on the

job. Learn the basic concepts and industry jargon. It is no secret that women get charged more for vehicle repairs. Why is that? According to Lisa Coxon, editor at LowestRates.ca, it comes down to presumed knowledge. Women are presumed to have less knowledge of vehicle repairs than men. The same discriminatory practice happens in business every day. The buyers that are thought to have less understanding of the job and the industry are often quoted more money. The best way to combat this is to be knowledgeable.

2. Know exactly what you're looking for

Before meeting with anyone, make sure you know exactly what you are looking for and what your expectations are. Do you need a site where you can sell products, take appointments, host forums and webinars? Or do you only need a simple informational site?

Write down your expectations and make sure they're clear. Next, check out the websites of some of the top players in your industry and interact with the sites. See any elements you like? What about elements you don't like? Note them. Also, be ready with examples. I highly recommend visiting *awwwards.com*. Awwwards is a website where web development experts meet to honor originality and innovation on the web. Once there, search for your industry and see what some of the top websites look like. Bookmark them for later.

3. Utilize individuals rather than agencies

You'll find that people are the most incredible resource in your entrepreneurial journey. When it comes to long term projects, many freelancers, students, contractors, or even some hobbyists can provide you with work that rivals many companies and agencies at a fraction of the cost. These people are an entrepreneur's greatest weapon. But where do you find these weapons and how do you add them to your arsenal? On the internet, of course.

I have personally used sites like UpWork, Fiverr and PeoplePerHour, which provide a platform that gives businesses access to freelance workers.

Your next resource is college campuses. That's where you'll find countless soon-to-graduate students who are looking to boost their portfolios and experience before entering the workforce, and your project might just be the one they're looking for.

The reason individuals are a better choice than companies, in terms of pricing, is because they simply don't have the massive overhead and expenses like companies and agencies. The cost savings are passed down to you.

4. Get quotes – lots and lots of quotes

My most important tip thus far: *never go with the very first quote you are given*. Reach out to multiple service providers. You'll find that while prices will hover around a similar range, there will always be several people who can provide the same service at a much better cost. Once you have gotten a decent number of quotes, use them to pit contractors against each other! Don't hesitate to mention a lower-priced quote and see who is willing to provide a markdown. It is important to remember that it is incredibly rare for you to get the best price the first time. Everyone has their markup, and savvy negotiators know how to bring it down. It is worth mentioning, however, do not get carried away by cheaper alternatives. These could come at the expense of quality. On the other hand, costlier isn't always better. The key here is to find a sense of balance.

Once you've found your designer, vetted their work and arranged payment, don't forget to be involved in the development process.

WRITING IMPECCABLE COPY

Now, your website is done but, mind you; it's not ready. Any great marketer knows that content is always a crucial piece in building an audience. Content truly is king. This fact is the primary reason Instagram influencers fill their feeds with dozens of gorgeous and stylish photos. It is also why top YouTubers operate on a posting schedule.

The key to keeping your audience engaged is having content they can engage with. One of the simplest and most cost-effective content types is written content. In this section, I'll share how to produce written content for your website, also known as copy.

Copy refers to written marketing content used on your website, blog, in emails, or on social media to encourage readers to buy your product.

·········

Good Copy Can Sell Anything

The hardest part about writing copy is the fact that there is no structured process to follow. Copy will significantly differ based on your niche and audience. When it comes to successful marketing copy, I've noticed that it is always produced by companies who understand that fact.

Kim Kardashian at the ShoeDazzle launch.

In 2009, reality television star **Kim Kardashian** co-founded a women's fashion subscription service called ShoeDazzle. The company, based in El

Segundo, California, featured an exclusive new collection of shoes, handbags and jewelry every month. Members were then presented with a link to a showroom featuring some of these items. Each item in the showroom was handpicked by a stylist based on the member's fashion preferences (which were established by having them take a quiz when they first signed up).

This business model required ShoeDazzle to rely heavily on email communications to inform members when designs were ready and direct members to their website each month. An aspect of those emails that frequently earned praise was the marketing copy. Aside from ShoeDazzle's celebrity recognition, high-quality photography and the company's commitment to price all their items below $40, the company's marketing team employed imaginative and witty copy to attract women to their site every month.

When ShoeDazzle members opened their inbox,

they were greeted with subject lines that read, *"Open with caution - these styles are hot."*

This style of copy worked well because ShoeDazzle knew and understood their audience: women, ages 21-35, seeking shoes that were either elegant, sexy or edgy, but most importantly, eye-catching.

Their website also utilized creative language that seemed to speak directly to their audience:

ShoeDazzle created a new way to spoil women who love fashion and lust after shoes, because we believe style is a way of life, deeply personal, and should always be fun. Today, millions of women get their personalized fashion fix from us, with access to top trends, style inspiration, and world-class service.

SOURCE: SHOEDAZZLE

Pay attention to the phrases that I highlighted. Those are some of the terms that made

ShoeDazzle's copy so interesting and effective.

Here's why they work:

Phrase 1 *spoil women* – this term plays on their audience's instinctive desire to be treated excellently. It brings to mind feelings of being pampered and puts into the reader's head the idea that they too deserve to be spoiled.

Phrase 2 *lust after shoes* – the term reinforces who exactly ShoeDazzle is catering to. Rather than using a standard phrase like "women who love shoes," the term "lust after shoes" emphasizes that ShoeDazzle is catering to trendy consumers.

Phrase 3 *millions of women* – this phrase inserts "the herd" concept to build consumer trust. It indirectly says to the reader, "Millions of women are already using us, why aren't you?" This is a meticulous tactic for inducing the fear of missing out. While your business might not yet be able to boast those numbers, phrases like "hundreds of…" or even "dozens of…." can be just as effective.

In your business, get to know your audience before writing for them. Employ writing styles that are both professional, personal, and creative. Writing good copy is a skill that is learned over time and mastered through practice.

A fantastic resource for entrepreneurs looking to connect with their audience using marketing copy is The Copy Cure, an online copywriting course by bestselling author Marie Forleo.

PART 2

INFLUENCING PERCEPTION

How will people perceive your company? In this part, I'll provide you with strategies you can implement to command a more massive presence in your industry. In the end, you will have added to your small business toolkit: a growing social following, a corporate telephone system, and the ability to serve your clients 24/7 — just like the big guys. But most importantly, you'll gain a high-value business presence that will have your startup looking like it belongs in the next Fortune 500 list. After implementing these same techniques in other businesses, I have been told by owners that they've received inquiries from other individuals about franchising with their venture, not knowing they themselves are just small business operators.

·········

Controlling The Narrative

Daymond John, Founder and CEO of FUBU

Fashion entrepreneur **Daymond John** started his FUBU clothing line (the name means *For Us By Us*) in 1992. He knew he would need to influence the way the market perceived his company if he wanted to stand a chance against industry juggernauts like NIKE and Reebook.

After numerous successful sales events, like selling out over a quarter million samples at Las Vegas' MAGIC Men's Apparel store, the then 23-

year-old founder ran a classified advertisement in the New York Times and landed technology giant Samsung as an investor.

Aside from Samsung's vote of confidence, John found other ways to influence how his clothing line was perceived by way of affiliation.

In 1999, rapper James Todd Smith, better known as LL Cool J, gave John's clothing line its most significant publicity boost to date. LL Cool J incorporated the company's phrasing "For Us By Us" in the rap lyrics of a commercial for a competitor, GAP Inc. According to a company executive, Keith Perrin, the GAP's production team was unaware of the phrase's meaning and had no idea it was referencing a competing brand until after the advertisement had aired. But perhaps even more beneficial to John and the team at FUBU, was the fact that LL Cool J wore a FUBU hat during the commercial. This paved the way for FUBU to be perceived as a brand with street cred and gave it broad acceptance within hip hop music.

Cool J repping FUBU in GAP's Commercial

Although the newfound fame of John's clothing line might have seemed like the result of fortune, it was far from. John had long had the vision of making sure that FUBU was perceived as more than just a clothing brand, but also a hip hop stand-out. At an APB Speakers conference in 2017, John said to the audience that at the time, he thought, "No matter what, I'm going to be a part of that world." Although he couldn't make a career from hip hop due to his lack of talent, he knew that FUBU could be a vehicle into that world, as long as he was able to influence perception. At this point, it is probably worth mentioning that it was John himself who pitched FUBU to rapper LL Cool J.

"I knew he could hook me up with Russell Simmons and everybody else," the founder stated.

In Part 3 of this book, I will reveal how you can bring in endorsements to make your small business stay relevant. But before that can be done, you'll need to give the impression that you are worthy of being endorsed. That is what we will be doing here in Part 2, building a bridge to get you there.

CRAFTING A SOCIAL PRESENCE

The very first step in the journey of perception is making sure people can see you. A hard reality is, if they don't see you, they aren't thinking of you. Nowadays, the best way to get eyes on your brand is via social media. In my playbook, the first rule of social media is to build your profiles on the platforms that your audiences are on. It's no secret that different platforms attract different audiences.

In most cases, the LinkedIn professional belongs to a completely different demographic as opposed to the Instagram influencer. It's not an exact science, but it holds weight. While you're more than welcome to set up shop on multiple platforms, you'll find that you will gain better results by focusing on the platforms that best fit your niche.

Establishing your presence on the right platforms, to begin with, will help your company's social clout grow faster while you build connections with people who genuinely care about what you have to offer.

On the next page, you'll find a chart you can use to see which platforms to focus your attention on.

MARKETING RESOURCE

Here are some of the most popular social networking sites, their reach, as well as a general overview of what niche each platform is best suited for.

Platform	Reach	Niches
facebook	1.4 Billion	Entertainment, Family, Relationships
twitter	600 Million	News, Public Relations, Technology and Finance
Instagram	200 Million	Retail Travel, Lifestyle, Fashion, Food, Fitness
Linked in	600 Million	Consulting, Professional Services, B2B, Human Resources
Pinterest	70 Million	Arts & Crafts, Home Décor, Fashion, DIYs
YouTube	2 Billion	In-person Services, Construction, How-to's

Source: accion.org

Once you have found the right platform(s) to build your brand on, what you'll be doing is using your social media pages as your company's "offices." The goal here is to use those so-called offices to attract people and then send them to your website. Just think back to Corcoran in Part 1. She used those classified ads, billboards, and word-of-mouth marketing to attract her customers back to *Corcoran.com*.

What you're doing now is similar to that strategy. It's just been adapted for the digital age. So rather than billboards and classifieds, you're using social media.

·········

Building Appealing Social Media Profiles

You've now got an impactful logo, a professional website, and impeccable copy. You've also figured out which social media platforms you'll be targeting. Now, it's time to build your company's social media profiles. When creating your social media profiles, consistency and quality should be first in your mind. The layout and styling of your business's page will be judged far heavier than that of a personal page. Don't skip this section.

Remember what I said about your logo being your company's face? On your personal social media profiles, the first thing people want to see is your face. For your company profile, the first thing people will want to see is your logo. After all, it's what they'll use to identify your brand. Depending on the layout of your logo, you might need to get it modified for use as your profile picture. Take a look at this example using Air Canada's Twitter profile:

Air Canada's complete logo looks minuscule if it were to be used as their profile picture, so instead, the airline opted for just using their maple leaf emblem. Apply this same concept to your brand. If your logo's layout doesn't lend itself to the profile picture ratio, use a modified version that features a recognizable brand emblem. As a rule of thumb, I'd suggest making your logo take up about 80% of the profile photo space. This guarantees recognition.

Still on the topic of recognition: consider using the same username across all your company's social media platforms. Try not to use something like @Example on one platform and @ExampleLtd on another. Be consistent. Using the same handle will not only help your audiences recognize you, but it will also help score you points with search engines. But how do you know if your chosen handle is available on all the platforms you'll be setting up shop? Well, you could create an account on each site and check to see if the handle is available. But that can be time-consuming. This is where a company like *Namechk.com* comes in. Namechk, created by David Goose and Jeremy Woertink, allows you to check if the domain and social media handles for your desired name are still available. Rather than review each social media site individually, Namechk searches close to 100 different social media sites, all at the same time.

While it is undoubtedly true that everyone starts at zero in the world of social media, in that same world, the value of social proof rivals that of gold. It's like the saying, "The rich get richer and the poor get poorer", but on social media, I like to say, "The trendy get trendier…"

As contradictory as it might sound, if you want to gain followers, you'll need followers.

While there are many black hat ways of accomplishing this, like buying followers or transferring account ownership, one low-cost white hat method I have found is this:

Whenever you make a new social media post, SPONSOR IT! The second your post goes live, click that "Boost Post" button to run a mini ad campaign. Run your ad for 12 to 24 hours. The idea behind this timeframe is your post will be receiving likes and engagements within a short time of being posted. Once the ad ends, your post will still have the engagement metrics (the likes, comments, etc.). When other users see that your post has been engaged with, they are more likely to take an interest in your post. They are more likely to engage with it. The next step is to return the favor and interact with all those who have interacted with your post. Like their comments, follow them, and comment on their posts. Since they took the initial interest in your post, this shows that the user has some level of pre-existing interest in your brand or content and will frequently follow you back. Of course, not everyone who interacts with your profile, and you theirs, will convert into a follower, but many will. Depending on your ad budget, approach and time commitment, in a few weeks of following this method, you can expect to see your following grow by the hundreds.

LAUNCH COMMUNICATION SYSTEMS

How does that saying go again? The one about trying to make a relationship work? Oh right... "Communication is key."

Communication will also be key when interacting with your customers. Large companies know this. That is why they invest millions in customer service, hiring large teams, running call centers and opening multiple locations. It is all so that their customers can have access to them. Why? They know that this is a pivotal element in their operations.

·········

Delivering Service That Wows

Zappos customer support offices in Las Vegas, Nevada.

Zappos, a popular Las Vegas-based online retailer with the stated objective "to live and deliver WOW," has mastered their communication system, and their clients love them for it. Zappos provides the customer with access to what they call their "Loyalty Team" 24 hours a day, seven days a week. Clients can get in touch with Zappos through at least five different mediums, including phone, live chat, social media and email.

Small businesses should aim to implement at least three reliable communication channels to strengthen the customer experience and remain competitive in their sector.

You might be asking, "But does my small business really need a corporate-style communication system?" Remember the point in Part 1 about utilizing your "low-key time" wisely?

When your company starts to attract larger audiences and you begin to serve more clients, you'll be faced with the reality that if you weren't able to manage the few you had, you would probably fail to manage the many. This is among the top reasons why oftentimes, businesses that are catapulted into the limelight suddenly nosedive after being overwhelmed. Take for instance, the wearable tech startup, Pebble. Pebble raised way too much funding too quickly, attracted much attention, and received higher demand than they could handle. They never built the infrastructure to sustain the needs of their customers. Pebble was discontinued in December of 2016. Competitor Fitbit acquired much of its assets and workforce, including software engineers and product testers.

Without a well-designed communication infrastructure, you can ruin relationships with clients. This will tarnish your image, reduce customer faith and destroy any goodwill towards your business overall. In this section, I will take you through some straightforward ways that you can have an intact communication infrastructure that will not only serve your clients well, but also take a page from Zappos' playbook and deliver a service that wows.

For small businesses, you shouldn't spend a fortune hiring people like customer care agents, client managers and staff supervisors. Instead, you should invest in affordable systems to connect with your clients. I'm talking about methods that utilize technology, ease-of-use as well as self-service.

1. Live Chat

This has swiftly become one of the most widely adopted ways of interacting with your clients. Technology has blurred the line between working hours and personal hours. A team of one can quickly reply to a visitor on your site via various apps like Drift, HubSpot Live Chat, Pure Chat, or LiveChat.com – just to name a few in an endless list.

These companies have made their platforms so straightforward and mobile that you can have their applications on your smartphone, and when someone needs something on your website and interacts with the live chat, you will be notified and be able to reply like you would a text message.

Additionally, these services allow you to set opening hours and collect lead data like email addresses and phone numbers before the chat, as well as let visitors leave a message if they contact you outside of opening hours.

Live chat has highlighted the importance of having a website, rather than just a physical location. Who can visit your office at 10:00 PM? With a website, someone can be searching online for your product or service and interact with your company at any time.

2. Electronic Mail (yeah, email)

Despite being created in the 1970s, email is still one of the best ways to build a relationship between your business and your customers. This is evidenced by how much the 'email marketing' industry has been on the rise in the past several years, partly thanks to companies like MailChimp and Constant Contact, which allow you to design and send email newsletters to clients.

Having a section where your visitors and clients can submit their emails and queries is not only a marketing tool, but also the foundation for building client relationships.

Keep your clients up to date with email newsletters featuring sales, news and events coupled with that impeccable copy that we looked at in Part 1. Having a professional weekly or monthly company newsletter helps clients view your company as an active organization. Instead of having them seeking you out on social media or blogs, a newsletter comes directly into their inbox.

Furthermore, another clever approach to boosting your company's persona is through the use of more than one email address for different inquiries. For instance, have one email address be billing@example.com and another be support@example.com. To easily accomplish this, use Email Forwarding. In most cases, wherever you bought your website domain will provide free email forwarding. With email forwarding set up, whenever a client emails one of those addresses, their message will be sent to your company's main inbox where you can view and reply to it. This is a brilliant method if you want to add that extra touch of professionalism. Rather than have clients email that free Gmail account, have them send their message to your branded email address. This is an understated way to come across as being more professional.

Next, when you receive an email from a visitor or a client, ensure that you respond to it with the most relevant response and in the fastest possible time. I always advise business owners to go the extra mile by predicting why visitors may need to contact them (check out the *Knowledge Is Power* activity on Page 75 for more details). Furthermore, make use of email templates to help reduce response times. I've often discovered that in customer service, it is best to under-promise and over-deliver. Set up an auto-reply email letting customers know that you got their message and will respond within a day or two, then surprise them and respond even sooner. It's slight, but it all builds up to delivering service that wows.

3. Social Media

Having already examined the importance of social media to your business, I've seen the need to put it here as a communication tool. Though social media is often perceived as an informal communication medium, you cannot remain oblivious to it.

When people find your business on social media, it is easier for them to interact via the instant messaging features than to look up your email address, website, or phone number.

Therefore, giving apt replies by having someone checking the inbox can be a low-cost, quick and non-technical way to facilitate quality communication.

4. Phone

Although many businesses have now fully embraced the methods mentioned above, person-to-person calls remain one of the most authentic communication methods. You can connect on a more personal level via a phone call. Voice gives you some non-verbal cues like a person's tone, which increases the efficacy of communication. To get the most out of your communication efforts, you should be able to not only listen to your customers, but feel them. A phone call gives you a chance to take care of your business on the spot. When talking, you solve everything in real-time and get feedback immediately, unlike emailing where you press send and hope for a quick reply from the receiver.

In sticking with the theme of this book, your phone system can be one of the best tools to enhance your company's image. Services like Grasshopper, RingCentral and Amazon's Contact Center Solutions will allow your company to set up a memorable and professional appearance using toll-free and local vanity numbers (e.g., 555-123-VOTE). Toll-free numbers help your business look the part, while vanity numbers are memorable and have been the cornerstone of many famous brands like 1-800-Flowers, 1-800-Got-Junk and even J.G. Wentworth with 877-Cash-Now.

Having an auto-attendant with programed departments (akin to "Press 1 for *Sales* or 2 for *Support*") helps fashion your company as being larger than it is.

Why not have your auto-attendant address common inquiries like opening hours and locations?

CUSTOMER SERVICE ACTIVITY
Knowledge is Power

For this activity, you will need to examine your company from an outsider's perspective. You've got to ask, "If I were a potential customer, what aspects of my business would need clarification?" The fact is, it is not always easy to answer these questions as an insider. You're already an expert in your business. But after completing this activity, not only will you be able to answer those types of questions, you'll also have a practical tool that you can use to propel your customer relations.

For the next 30 days, you or your team will note down every question or concern a customer has had and how you responded to that concern. At the end of the 30 days, look through your notes. Which questions appeared three or more times? Highlight them. Those questions are what you'll consider being your Frequently Asked Questions (FAQs). These will be invaluable in your client communications. Use them to draft email templates, canned chat responses, and even to train new hires in your company. You can even use them to create FAQ sections on your website.

As time goes by and your operations evolve, come back to this activity to expand those Frequently Asked Questions. Once you have enough of them (say fifty to a hundred), check out platforms like Zendesk, Document360, or Helpjuice, to create a searchable knowledge base for customers to assist themselves with those common inquiries. This will ease the pressure on your team as well as foster a level of independence among your clients.

SETTING UP MULTIPLE DEPARTMENTS

A business with multiple departments will undoubtedly command the assumption of being much larger as opposed to a one-man-band. Why? Companies with departments often seem to be 'bigger' and more efficient. My goal here is to help your business adopt that model while still being a small venture.

Most small business owners think that their business is too small to have organizational departments. The truth is, no matter the size of your business, if you want to operate effectively, then you'll need to set up departments. Whether you are in retail, sales, manufacturing, or professional services, departments are essential to making your operations more manageable.

As a small business owner, you're likely captaining the ship yourself, but as time progresses, it will be important to launch departments. You might be examining this from the financial point-of-view and thinking that it will cost your business a fortune. However, the main goal here is ensuring that if your small business is at the stage to set up departments, you are strategic and ready.

You might be asking, *"How do I know if my business is ready?"*

The answer: *you meet one of these requirements:*

(a) You don't have the time.

You're busy with other aspects of your business. Think of it like hiring a house cleaning service. You could certainly do the job yourself, but your time might be better spent doing something else. It's the same in your business. You can delegate some tasks if you're busy with more important ones, like the tasks directly bringing revenue into your company.

(b) You can't do it yourself.

Businesses require multiple moving parts, from accounting to marketing, customer service to sales. For instance, you might own a flower shop and be the best florist in town, but by no means are you an accountant. But despite that you'll still have to complete taxes, pay suppliers, track expenses, and create financial statements.

I will take you through a process that you can follow to establish micro-departments in your small business. Not only will this provide the outward appearance of being a larger player, but it will also give you a functioning advantage.

Let's start with what I consider to be essential departments in every business.

1. Operations

Every operational business has this department. They might not label it as the "operations department," but it's there. This department encompasses all the moving parts that are responsible for serving customers and fulfilling their needs.

This department is the engine of your business. It ensures that the company is producing the goods and services it promised, at the time it promised and at the quality it promised. Smooth operation leads to happy customers who will, in turn, refer others to your company. These referrals convert into more satisfied customers. That's the best way to ensure that your business is growing and is profitable. To be successful, this department needs to maximize production with the little resources available to most small businesses.

Every day you go to work in your company, this

department is open for business and is most likely headed by you. But at some point, you'll need to recruit people or even a single person to join hands with you and continue from where you have been operating solely. While hiring, ensure that you hire a *strong* person. You should go for an ambitious person who is open-minded and has room for growth. You will not remain a small business forever. Therefore, getting someone open to change and who can manage other employees is best.

One of the easiest ways to move from a one-man-army to a team is to document processes. What are the things you do daily? I'm talking about essential tasks, like data entry, ringing up customers or inventory management. Document them. It will make training new additions to your company easy and serve as a reference guide when you or the person you put in charge are not around. This tip doesn't just apply to operations; it applies to every sector of your business.

2. Marketing & Advertising

After all, this book is called **The Marketing Fallacy**, so the marketing and advertising department making a list should not surprise you. This is the department responsible for your *brand*. It will drive customers to you.

Having written this book to showcase the value of portraying your business as a large company, it should indeed be noted that as a small business, you won't be able to staff a large marketing team with a massive budget and complex team structure. If you could, you probably wouldn't need this book in the first place. But you don't need all of that to create a killer marketing and advertising department. One person can run this department comfortably. You'll need to hire an IT literate individual with knowledge in marketing and promotions. The reason this person must be

IT savvy and with some technical background is due to the ever-changing business landscape. As business and life, in general, continue to move online you need people on your team who will traverse this new terrain. Platforms like Google Skillshop, LinkedIn and edX, offer low-cost and, sometimes, free courses that you can use to train new hires.

Your client demand and workload will always dictate the number of people to place in each department, but it is wise to start with one, train and perfect them, then grow slowly and expand as required.

3. Financial & Administration

This is the third and final part of what I consider the three essential departments of any business. This department is responsible for overseeing all financial and office-related services. The individual in charge of this department should be organized, smart, efficient, and possess the integrity needed to handle the most sensitive business information - your finances.

This person will work together with the other two departments to ensure that the cost of procedures is catered for. They monitor and analyze costs, income and budgets. The finance and administration departments also help with implementing ways to run all operations at the lowest possible cost, in an attempt to ensure maximum profitability. This department will also handle management, procurement and bookkeeping, as well as disburse salaries to staff and can oversee primary HR duties.

Once you have established this basic three-division structure, your business will be ready to tackle its next milestones better. You will also be in a position to expand and form new divisions as your business grows. With time, you may see the need to establish other departments or customize those already formed.

Now, remember that email forwarding tip? Here is where it's most helpful. Create email addresses for just about each of your new departments, i.e., operations@example.com. Do you recall the advice about using auto-attendant phone features? Use it to give each department its own extension. You can also create custom business cards for you and your team with their title and department.

Ashley Smith

Sales

T: 1-888-555-4321 (opt. 2)
E: sales@yourcmpany.com

An example business card using departments and extensions.

These are subtle yet effective ways of presenting your company as a well-run firm. Implemented correctly, they can help you command respect and trust and set your small business apart.

BEING OPEN 24 HOURS A DAY

Previously, I mentioned how this digital era had blurred the line between working hours and personal hours. But when I talk about being open 24 hours a day, I don't mean that if you have a physical location you should not close it. What I mean is you being within reach of your customers on a 24/7 basis. That possibility has been made easy thanks to our digital realm. As previously discussed, you can interact with your customers through your website, social media, live chat and via email.

Interacting with your customers doesn't mean that you're always physically in reach. Research from HubSpot shows that 9 out of 10 people contacting your business consider an "immediate" response as being necessary. As an affordable way of meeting this expectation, you can have a bot on-site that directs visitors while providing them with answers to your frequently asked questions. This gives clients the "immediate" response they seek, even if it's an automated one.

Let's say you're in the manufacturing industry, and a customer has purchased your product recently. They should be able to access you anytime they need help with your product. It doesn't matter whether it is day or night. As long as they're using it, they expect you to be there to help. That's why most large companies that create products with some learning curve often have a blog with "how-to" posts that are written to guide customers on the usage of their product. Your bot can direct customers to that blog, giving them the most relevant link based on their questions.

·········

Automation Isn't Just For Tech Giants

PayPal headquarters in San Jose, California.

PayPal is a perfect example of a service provider with these features. You chat with a bot and the bot replies to you with the most relevant answers and links to their support blog and help forum.

Nowadays, many businesses are using automation in some way to keep in touch with their customers. There are specific tools, some free and others paid, that can help you do the same, even in your small business. These tools allow you to connect apps, automate tasks and systematize workflows, increasing productivity and accessibility.

Zapier is a widely known tool that can help you in automated workflow. There are similar tools like Integromat, Microsoft's Flow, and Workato.

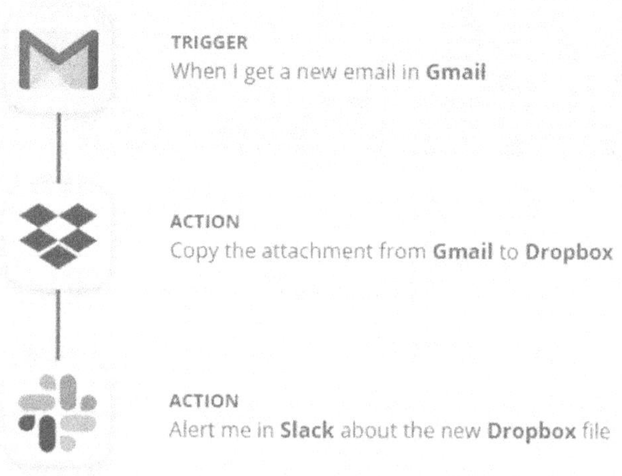

Example of how Zapier works (zapier.com)

Using tools like Zapier, you can create automated email replies, notify team members about client requests, add new clients to your database, and so much more. The best part is many of these tools detect customer information and can produce personalized responses.

Another way to ensure your business is always accessible to the customer is through post-purchase follow ups. Following up with customers who have purchased from you is a fantastic way to connect, gain feedback and help resolve unvoiced concerns. Your best marketers are the people who have bought or used your service in the past. The rise of online review sites has made it an expected requirement that people read reviews before making a purchase. Therefore, following up on your past customers' experience is highly critical.

Regardless of how helpful automation might be, it doesn't entirely replace the value of human interaction. Companies like HelpSquad and Norgress hire and train customer service contractors and sales agents on your behalf and service your website 24/7 (more on outsourcing shortly). Before deciding whether or not you need real people working around the clock, you need to analyze the kind of customers you have and your business's core offerings. For example: some businesses offering time-sensitive services at high demand, like Airbnb and JetBlue. These companies operate with round-the-clock support staff, and the reasons make sense. People are always traveling. Travel is a 24-hour industry. Those travelers need where to stay. So, JetBlue provides 24/7 customer support because of the industry, while Airbnb offers it because of its customer base.

Secondly, you need to know where your customers are located. With the advent of the internet, a local business might have a global customer base, which means their customers will all be in different time zones. When deciding on staffing 24/7, you should also ask yourself how this will help you in terms of competition. In many cases, it could provide you with a competitive advantage if you are available all the time, while your competition is not.

While you can approach staffing from the typical or more established routes, I aim to help you follow the most appropriate and cost-saving paths. With that said, there are two ways in which you can expand your support hours at a fraction of the cost:

1. Contracting a Remote Workforce

A large band of entrepreneurs now recognize the need for virtual assistants or remote workers. Consider hiring someone within a different time zone, such that their working hours are during your nighttime. With the correct training, they can offer support to your customers. When they are not interacting with customers, have them complete small duties and tasks like calendar management, adding customers to your database and more.

When tackling the hiring process, you can use a platform like EasyHire.me or Jobma to spontaneously conduct multiple applicant interviews without having to reach out to each applicant individually, arrange an interview and meet with them. Hiring is perhaps one of the most stressful tasks in business. But these services, which start at $1 per interview, take much of the stress out of hiring by having a computer conduct interviews for you. I have found applicants love it because they do their interviews at any time and are not burdened with the act of sitting face-to-face with someone.

2. Utilizing Outsourcing

Partnering with a customer support outsourcing organization can be an efficient way of making sure that your customers reach you and get the help they need at any time of the day. It is also relatively cheap because they work with many companies; thus, you can experience what is called the *economies of scale* effect when it comes to their pricing. However there is a considerable downside to this. Since these companies are working with multiple other businesses, don't expect the level of support provided to your customers to be in-depth. For a small business with little technicalities, outsourcing is the way to go. If your business requires a more in-depth level of support, like technology companies, outsourcing will not be your best bet.

PART 3

MAINTAINING RELEVANCE

You must have heard of big companies that existed, but are nowhere to be seen today. Do you have a company on your mind that followed that path? Maybe MySpace, PayLess, Sears or even BlackBerry? For me, the one that always comes to mind is Pan American Airways, aka Pan Am. The airline was once the most extensive international carrier in the United States. In 1970, it flew over 11 million passengers to 86 different countries. By 1991, Pan Am was no more. What happened?

The truth is, all businesses come to be no more at some point. The Googles, Amazons and Apples of today won't be the ones of tomorrow. Similarly, those of us living now won't be the ones living decades from now. But just like how diet, exercise and a positive mindset can help extend a person's life, the right planning and execution can help a company extend its life. In this chapter, I will show you ways to help your small business remain relevant to your market. From endorsements to public relations, as well as establishing safeguards, each will help to support the continuity of your venture.

STAYING IN THE KNOW

Being up to date on the emerging trends within your market may sound like a minor and somewhat basic business feature; however, it is one that has made giants flounder while underdogs flourish. So pay close attention.

CORPORATE HISTORY ACTIVITY
The Brands of Yesteryear

*For this activity, try to recall popular brands that seemed to stand at the top of their markets, yet failed. Try to come up with at least five of them. Next, once you have a list of companies in hand, conduct a Google search for each using the term: **"Why did _________ fail?"***

What reasons are discovered? Uninformed management, lack of interest from the public, insufficient marketing, or inability to compete? Is there anything you can learn from these failures?

·········

When Innovators Fail To Innovate

Another company that fell down the well was **Kodak**. Founded in 1889, it became a giant in the photography industry during the 1970s. In 2012, it filed for bankruptcy.

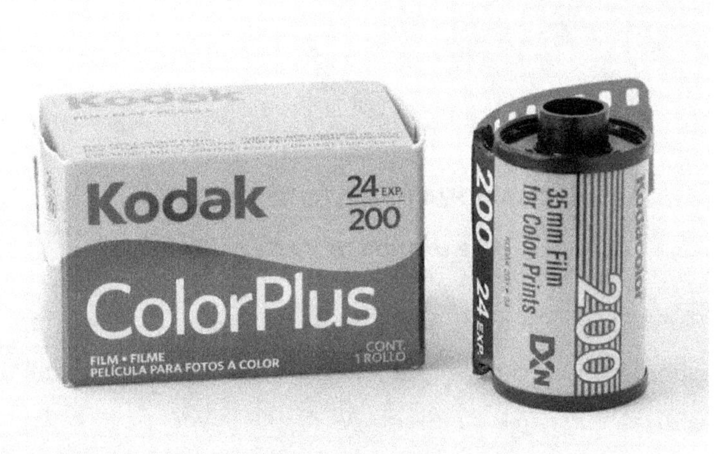

Kodak filed for Chapter 11 bankruptcy in 2012.

Kodak dominated the photography market in the 20th century. The company was founded by entrepreneur George Eastman who was planning for a vacation in 1888. While preparing to leave, he was tasked with taking photos. Back then, taking photos meant carrying a huge box, chemical bottles, films and a gigantic camera. Disappointed with that reality, he canceled his trip and spent the time looking for a more convenient way to take a photo without hauling all that equipment. Eastman later launched the Kodak Camera. It was significantly lighter and cheaper, with a price tag of $25. The camera came with a 100-frame film. When the roll was full, the buyer would mail it back to Kodak, which would charge $10 to develop the photos.

By 1902, Eastman and his Kodak Company had sold 80% of the world's celluloid films. Kodak forced its competitors to either adapt or leave the market. Kodak remained on top and was always developing new products, including the color film in the 1920s.

Most folks believe Kodak's downfall began when they failed to embrace the digital advent. This holds some truth, but what many don't realize is, Kodak was the first inventor of the digital camera. The real mistake that Kodak made was continuing to push their sales efforts towards films and camera accessories. They simply did not give the required attention to the market's interest in digital cameras. Why? Because they thought it would never be the mainstream camera — a big mistake.

With the household name level of recognition gained from their early patented invention, they could easily have leveraged their brand while endorsing the new digital revolution - but they did not.

Eventually, new players who embraced the digital era joined the game. They produced new cameras, new technologies and introduced brand-new consumer options that were far more user friendly. With these new digital cameras, there was no longer a need for films and Kodak's main sales driver was redundant.

From Kodak's story, we can learn this: always be ready to adapt. Transform and adjust your business strategy and model. You should also be prepared to shift from the advantage you are experiencing to the unknown.

In your small business, you should ensure that you know the emerging trends within your market. Don't be frightened by the idea of stepping outside of your comfort zone. By this, I mean the place you are selling most and venturing into what you think is the next significant movement, the unknown. Therefore, seeking out new trends and market developments should be your initiative as an owner. Employees may hardly tell you what they frankly think, and you can't blame them. The sad truth is, many businesses don't operate in an atmosphere where worker feedback is appreciated. This highlights the need to have a close relationship with your staff, contractors and remote workers. They can be an invaluable source of knowledge if you let them.

However, the most essential source of information is your customers. Build relationships with them. This will ensure that you tailor your services to suit them. Additionally, having mentioned in the previous Part the importance of social media, it's worth noting that you can get lots of information about your market right there. So, stalk it now and then. Furthermore, ensure you respond to the issues of your industry, whether that means reacting to market feedback or investing some time and money into the latest market trends. The objective is to stay relevant.

When you obtain feedback from customers, you should pay careful consideration to it and act fast to implement whatever needs to be implemented. If you don't, they'll seek another company. Remember, the world is moving fast. Failure to implement solutions swiftly means you will be replaced promptly.

·········

A Blueprint for Remaining Germane

Branson speaks at a Virgin Mobile event

Richard Branson, the head of Virgin Group, in an interview, once revealed that 25% of his time is spent trying to learn new endeavors and everything that needs to be known before launching them.

Whenever you implement, don't stop there, continue the search for more insights. Trends are always changing. You should too.

BUILDING A PR MACHINE

Branson, who has over 400 companies and nearly 70,000 employees worldwide, became well-known thanks to not only his successes in entrepreneurship, but also his publicity stunts. He once did a rather bizarre thing that led to him becoming a celebrity of sorts and a popular subject in the media's eye. In 1985, Branson attempted to cross the Atlantic Ocean on board a powerboat. Although he capsized and was saved by an RAF helicopter, he drew widespread media coverage for his attempts. The following year, in 1986, this time with a sailing expert, he not only did it, but he also beat the record by crossing the ocean in three days, eight hours and 31 minutes. In 1991, he crossed the Pacific from Japan to Arctic Canada using a balloon.

These daredevil stunts made Virgin Group a household name. Many publications termed the CEO of the Virgin Group among the greatest risk-takers of all time. This recognition helped in the growth of his companies, particularly his airline Virgin Atlantic. All these stunts are Branson's ways of marketing his company. This affirms that Branson understands the value of PR. A good PR story, according to Branson, is better than a front-page ad.

While I'm not urging you to follow his exact course, I am trying to let you know how important PR is to your business. At the beginning of this book, I mentioned how important first impressions are. This does not overrule the second and subsequent impressions. You cannot grow your small business without promoting it, and nothing works best like press coverage.

PR has proven to have higher conversion rates than advertising. A majority of people will trust your business if they find its story in the media, rather than if they simply see an ad.

There is no shortage of PR firms. You could always

hire one to help kick start your public relations journey, but I have found that they simply charge you for many things you can do yourself. You should take some time to get your business's name and brand out to as many people as possible, especially those in your target audience. In this section, I will show you how you can create your very own PR machine that gets results while being much more affordable than hiring a firm.

The right press coverage will help you increase your sales and get new customers faster than any other medium. There are many strategies you can employ to ensure your company's name gets out there. Thankfully, these strategies don't require you to cross the Atlantic.

Here's a breakdown of how you can build your own highly effective PR machine.

1. Refine & Perfect, Before Seeking Attention

Many companies put much of their effort into

getting PR without recognizing that PR could be detrimental. Before you attract attention to your business you have to put things in order. Think of it like tidying up before the guests arrive.

"There is no such thing as bad publicity."

That is a lie. If you did not use the time before that big break to create a firm foundation for your business, any publicity could trigger your downfall – even good publicity. Think back to Pebble as an example. It is for this reason that I emphasized the importance of building your foundation first. Remember, it's best to do the work when no one is watching. Once you've had an audience's attention and lost it, it's difficult to regain it. Plenty of public relations agencies will not tell you this because they are just looking for their next client.

2. Conduct Your Research

This involves getting more information about your buyers, their lifestyle, interest and activities to determine how to reach them best. Doing market research also lets you know the emerging trends in your industry, what your prospects need and why they choose a certain product over others. Whilst some companies pay to conduct market research using the help of experts, data analytics firms and research institutes, this isn't the most feasible pathway for a small business. Despite that, getting this information is crucial to constructing your public relations strategy.

Research helps determine which tools to utilize, which publications to pitch to, which events to attend and which contacts to build.

Two main types of research can be conducted.

Primary Research

This is getting firsthand information from your customers. In this case, you focus on a small group (a focus group). Meet with them and interview them. Your aim is to get renewed details from the people you have already won over.

This is a highly beneficial strategy that is both low cost and effective and should be the first step when deciding to carry out any form of market research.

Secondary Research

This is the data you get through public records, market statistics, business journals, trend reports, and many other sources.

Use this type of research to keep up with your market and, specifically, your competitors.

Secondary research is the best source for

competitor information. Large companies have entire teams dedicated to monitoring market activity. For your small business, however, Google will be your monitoring team. Conduct searches related to your industry to discover new entries, industry news and events. Or better yet, set up what's called a Google Alert. It will notify you when new content appears on the web related to your specified term, in this case, your industry.

By the end of your market research, you should have various relevant findings to be used in the subsequent steps in your PR endeavors.

3. Write Your Brand's Story

A good story can make your entire business. The brain is more likely to remember stories than numbers and facts. Refer back to the brand stories section in Part 1 and reuse your answers to those questions to help expand the story of your brand. The objective is to put that story on paper in such a way that people desire to not only read it but also share it.

First, let me acknowledge that crafting that story can be a bit challenging, but getting it in writing can be even more of a struggle and a very time consuming one at that. So, if you aren't the best writer in the room, remember that there are freelancers all over who can help.

While writing your story, always remember that you are not just enticing readers, but aiming to build a relationship with them. Therefore, do not write about the successes only. Start with the challenges, your passion and your reason. Through this, people will connect emotionally with the protagonist, your brand, and they will come back to check on that protagonist.

But what if I told you that protagonist could also be you? Like the Virgin Group, numerous companies have been propelled into the limelight thanks to their founders. Maybe you're already popular, highly charismatic, influential, or just a really fascinating founder. Whatever it is, tying your brand with your company can be an easy way to boost your company's profile. If you can, have your company piggyback off you. Mention your company whenever possible. It could be on social media, in your bio, through YouTube videos, at social gatherings, or networking events. People who are interested in you will naturally be interested in whatever you're associated with.

As you begin forming your story, you will discover that there will be different iterations as your business evolves. Do not make it hard for your audience. Maintain a central message. This calls for consistency. Once you've found your angle, voice, and tone - stick to it. Do not contradict anything in your stories. Doing so could make your brand look phony, fake.

4. Take A Deep Breath. Now Pitch

Finally, you are ready to go public. I'm not talking about an IPO or stock market launch. I'm talking about pitching. Pitching is sending a letter, calling, or emailing journalists and bloggers, or even editors at newspapers or magazines, with the hope that they will be interested in your story and publish it to their readers. Depending on the publication, editors receive hundreds of pitches each day so, they may only choose the most relevant ones; those that are worth publishing. My suggestion is to pitch to journalists that are directly in your industry. And then *wait*.

Remember that publications and blogs are inundated with correspondence. So, it might be a few weeks before you get a reply. If your attempts go unanswered, as many will, there are still other ways you can slip your company into the media.

TACTICS FOR GETTING MEDIA FEATURES

Guest Posting

With this tactic, you'll be exploiting the concept of guest posting. Simply put, writing for someone else's blog, news website, or magazine.

You'll find a newsworthy story related to your industry and use it as your pitch instead of your business. If your post is accepted, you'll often receive a contributor page on the site. This page usually features your name, title, bio as well as links to your website and social media. Use this page to plug your company.

Mark Shaw

Founder & CEO of Example.com

Hey there, I'm Mark. I'm a businessman living in Los Angeles, California as well as the founder and CEO of **www.example.com**

An example of a Contributor Bio

Many sites will include these contributor bios at

the end of the article. Frequently, readers will check you out as well as your company after reading the article. This provides coveted exposure and acts as a tool for social proof.

How exactly do I land a guest post?

Use the next Marketing Resource as a guide. It contains a list of top sites that currently accept guest posts as well as a template email that I have used when reaching out for guest posting opportunities in my industry.

It is important to note that guest posting isn't a surefire method. However, news outlets, blogs, and magazines are ALWAYS looking for content their readers will love. If you can provide them that content, they'll publish it. And again, if you're not the best writer, there are always people you can hire to help. While focusing your efforts on larger publications will help with accomplishing the goal of making your small business appear larger, don't neglect smaller outlets like blogs.

MARKETING RESOURCE
Guest Posting Sites

Here are some publications that accept contributor or guest post as well as the niches they are best suited for:

- **Harvard Business Review**

  Visit: *www.hbr.org/guidelines-for-authors*

  Acceptable Niches:
  - o *Finance*
  - o *Negotiations*
  - o *Management*
  - o *Innovation*

- **Mashable**

  Visit: *www.mashable.com/submit*

  Acceptable Niches:
  - o *Technology*
  - o *Entertainment*
  - o *Culture*

- **Inc. Magazine**

  Email: *contributors@inc.com*

  Acceptable Niches:
  - o *Startups*
  - o *Money*
  - o *Leadership*

- **LifeHack.org**

  Visit: *www.lifehack.org/contribute*

  Acceptable Niches:

  - o *Spirituality*
  - o *Health & Wellness*
  - o *Motivation*

- **Inspiring Travelers**

  Visit: *www.inspiringtravelers.com/contact*

  Acceptable Niches:

  - o *Travel (of course!)*
  - o *Photography*
  - o *Food*

- **Web & Designers**

  Visit: *www.webanddesigners.com/writ-for-us*

  Acceptable Niches:

  - o *Graphic Design*
  - o *Digital Media*
  - o *Web Development*

- **ThriveGlobal**

  Email: *communityhelp@thriveglobal.com.*

  Acceptable Niches:

  - o *Family*
  - o *Community*
  - o *Work-life Balance*

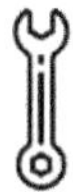

MARKETING RESOURCE

Guest Posting Email Template

Here is a copy of an email I have used when reaching out to publications. Feel free to modify and personalize it.

Hi **EDITOR NAME**,

Hope all is well!

My name is **FULL NAME**.

I'm writing you because a colleague of mine recently suggested that I reach out to your publication.

I am the founder and CEO of **COMPANY NAME** and have been a devoted reader of **PUBLICATION NAME**. I would love to share my knowledge and expertise with your readers.

Attached is an article that I would love to publish in **PUBLICATION NAME**, it's titled "How to Stay Creative When Working Remotely".

Let me know what you think!

Cheers,
FIRST NAME

Press Releases

A press release is a news item written in the hopes that media outlets will pick it up. It is perhaps one of the most important and most popular communication materials in PR. Some companies publish press releases on their sites for their audience to view, but the primary audience for press releases is editors and journalists who, in turn, publish them.

When writing press releases, ensure that the content therein is newsworthy. This content can be an upcoming event, a recent hire in your business, new promotions, philanthropic activities, or acquisitions. To distribute your company's Press Release, you can use distributors such as PRWeb or AccessWire.

Media Mentions

When it comes to media mentions, one service that hits the top of my list is HARO.

HARO stands for Help A Reporter Out, and it allows you to do just that. With HARO, you can register as a "source." Every week, you'll receive three emails daily (Monday to Friday), one at 5:35 AM, another at 12:35 PM, and a final one at 5:35 PM (EST). Each email contains requests from journalists, bloggers, news reporters and media outlets. If you're well-informed about any of the requested topics, you can reply to the request.

While there are certainly other ways of getting media mentions, what makes Help A Reporter Out a favorite of mine is, the journalists come to you.

Over 75,000 reporters use HARO. These reporters come from media outlets like ABC, Fox News, and The Wall Street Journal.

Book Writing

Another method is writing a book and publishing it under your company's name. For this, you will need to start an imprint. Simply put, an imprint is a publishing name that a company uses to publish works. You could name an imprint anything you'd like, but ideally, for this purpose, it should be an extension of your company's name. For instance: *Example Books* or even *Example Publishing*.

How exactly do I start an imprint and get a book published?

The process might differ slightly by country. Here in Canada, to start an imprint, you'll need to submit an application with LAC (Library and Archives of Canada). The submission is free, and your business only needs to be registered to apply. The best part is, your business does not even have to be in the book publishing industry.

Once your application is approved, you'll have access to the ISBN Canada online system to submit publications and generate International Standard Book Numbers (ISBNs). Once you have access to the system, generate your ISBN and get to work on your book. You can hire freelance editors, book cover designers, co-writers as well as typesetters and proofreaders along the way.

When your book is ready, the final step is finding a printer. You can use platforms like Tellwell, LuLu, or Ingram. Even Amazon has their own book printing platform. On the back of your book and the copyright page, you can include your company's logo, website and social media handles.

Once your book is in print, send copies to book reviewers and bloggers. If you're lucky, they'll feature your book, which will increase sales and in turn, raise awareness for your company. You can also gift your book to clients and business partners. The impression that your business published a book does wonders in fashioning it as a larger company.

Media Kits

Once you've gathered enough media mentions, guest posts, and press articles (about 10-15 I'd say), it's time to craft your media kit. Media kits all serve the same purpose. They are tools used by influencers, brands and organizations to raise their profile. They are a one-stop-shop for everything you need to know about a company, a brand, or an individual. They provide detailed information about the subject and showcase references to publications that they have previously been featured in. Having a media kit is a worthy PR goal.

A rule of thumb with media kits: the more attractive your kit, the more likely you are to capture your recipient's attention. So, don't be afraid to hire a designer! Just ensure that they adhere to consistency. Your brand color and company logo should be featured in your media kit.

I've found that media kits are a bit like books. Sure, eBooks are just fine, but to be honest, most folks *still* prefer physical books. Media kits are the same. The most effective ones are the physical ones. Print your kit. When it is done, you can mail it to business partners, journalists, editors, or media outlets.

A well-done media kit is an attention grabber. That's always the aim. They should make the recipient want to know more about you or the company. If your kit is successful in doing that, you can expect recipients to start reaching out to you. Therefore, your media kit should contain your contact details.

If you can't mail a physical copy of your media kit,

make sure to email it as a PDF file. Your business might not yet make the cut for radio and television broadcasts, but you might want to consider sending your media kit to podcasters and web series producers instead.

Sponsor or Host Events

One of the easiest and most fulfilling ways to make your small business seem like a big-time corporation is through event sponsorship. You can support an event by offering financial assistance, products or services. This is a go-to PR method for large firms, especially when the goal is to build trust with your client and prospects. Nowadays, many companies have embraced this method by sponsoring local events, charitable affairs, and social movements like Black Lives Matter or #MeToo. And it's easy to see why. It promotes corporate social responsibility while helping to catapult their brand.

It is important to note that sponsorship does not persuade the audience to make a purchase. If your goal is to use this method as a sales driver, don't. You'll be disappointed. What sponsorship does is portray your company as one that cares for the wellbeing of your society. Sponsorships shape consumers' attitudes, build brand awareness, increase reach, and generate media exposure while distinguishing yourself from your competitors.

A similar and more cost-effective alternative to sponsorship is starting a foundation that is closely related to your business. This is an excellent avenue for giving back and it's also an exceptional vehicle to get media attention.

GAINING ENDORSEMENTS

Getting an endorsement from an influential person can mean a lot for *any* business. It can instantly boost trustworthiness, sales and recognition considerably. Despite this, most small businesses may not have the budgets to afford a mention from Jay-Z or the Kardashians.

....

What is The Oprah Effect?

Oprah Winfrey endorsing Weight Watchers (WW.com)

According to the investment encyclopedia, Investopedia, **the *Oprah Effect*** (yup, that's an actual term) refers to the increase in sales that a company sees after receiving approval on *The Oprah Winfrey Show.* The talk show, which aired for over 25 years, ended in May of 2011. However, the conclusion of the show did not affect the *Oprah Effect.*

In 2015, Oprah invested in WW (better known as Weight Watchers) and joined the company's board of directors and took a prominent place in the company's marketing and advertising efforts as a media ambassador. Oprah's seal of approval hurled the company's stocks and added a reported one million new members within a year.

You do not have to get endorsements from the super famous to raise your company's profile. Even some social media influencers are indeed paid up to $50,000 for an Instagram post endorsing a business. Your company can still get endorsed even without spending a fortune on it. In this era of technology, you just need to think outside the box. There are many ways you can get endorsed.

Nowadays, public figure endorsements have become accessible to all businesses, regardless of their size. There are several ways to get a celebrity's endorsement. They all work, but they all require some patience. These are some of the most efficient ways to earn stellar endorsements for your brand.

1. Formulated Generosity

Everyone loves gifts. Instead of paying for endorsements, you can offer complimentary shipments of your product to potential endorsers. This will, in many cases, lead to an endorsement. You can even offer your services for free. For example, let's say a popular comedian announces, on his Instagram page, that he was moving to a new house. His fans were sending congratulatory messages, but an entrepreneur saw the best chance to leverage the celebrity for his brand. He sends a private message, stating that he owns a moving company and offered to handle everything to ensure that his relocation happens smoothly. When it was time, they arrived early and began the packing. The comedian who had saved a massive amount that he would have otherwise spent was happy. Consequently, he uploads a short video to his timeline stating his appreciation.

2. The Power of Equity

Equity does not necessarily have to be issued for cash. You can offer some ownership of your company in exchange for an endorsement.

When entrepreneurs enter the hit ABC television show Shark Tank, they do so in the hope of getting a cash investment in exchange for an equity share of their business. Longtime fans of the series may be aware of a frequently used quote by the investors, or Sharks as they are called. That quote is, "You're not just getting a partner, you're getting a Shark."

When entrepreneurs enter the Tank, if they are lucky enough to get a deal, they will also be instantaneously leaving with one of the most valuable endorsements in the North American small business realm, a Shark.

You don't have to land an appearance on Shark Tank to use the power of equity. Numerous prominent individuals will endorse your company in exchange for an equity share. The catch is, your company needs to have great future potential and an idea they believe in. If you do, you can leverage the shares to earn a valued collaborator and bragging rights.

3. Focusing On Your Industry

You might be thinking that the approval of a major household name is the best thing for your small business, but that could be a fallacy.

Depending on your business, an industry expert may be your finest bet.

To illustrate, an award-winning chef might very well be at the top of his game. He owns fine dining restaurants, multiple cooking books, major brand endorsements, and deals – yet despite his many accolades, he's only really well known within the culinary industry. Regardless of his lack of fanfare, his name holds weight.

Think of Yannick Alléno, Dan Barber, or Ferran Adrià. All are chefs at the top of their game, but they are most certainly not household names. Regardless, getting a stamp of approval from them would make any small business in the food industry a major participant.

While all of those men have brands and reputations to protect, and might not just liberally issue endorsements, it goes without saying that it would likely be cheaper and easier to get their endorsements, than it would be getting one from an A-list star. Therefore, you should strongly consider targeting individuals at the top of your industry who closely relate with your product or service.

How exactly do I get in touch with them?

The comedian example in point 1 demonstrates a satisfactory method: direct messaging via social media. Good in theory, but in actuality, most public figures do not frequently monitor their social media DMs. They're just too busy. While you may well be able to contact a local or lesser-known celeb on social media, this won't work for bigger stars. In that case, you're going to have to turn to the old fashioned method: reaching out to their publicist or manager.

A quick Google search will reveal which

management company most public figures belong to, and in some cases, their rep's information. If you found the company but can't locate their rep, here's a helpful tip:

On LinkedIn, search for the name of the management company. Next, send a connection request to a few relevant individuals at these companies. Make sure to give everyone a reason why they should accept your connection request. I'd suggest looking for commonalities like: Did you attend the same college? Are you a part of the same professional association? Do you have a few mutual connections? Whatever you do, don't send a blank request. Those are unlikely to be accepted.

I've found that the people who accept the connection request will also provide a follow-up message. Oftentimes, this leads to a brief discussion between you two. Avoid requesting anything during this initial conversation. Instead, reach back out in the future. Even if they don't remember you, the initial conversation will be there in the chat's history to spark their memory and they will be far more willing to engage with you a second time around. After getting introductory greetings out of the way, you could send something like this:

"I noticed your company represents _______. Would you be able to provide their publicist's contact? I have a project that I think would be of immense interest to them."

Alternatively, you can use IMDb Pro to discover the contact information of the management teams for different individuals. Since IMDb's information is oftentimes submitted by studios and agencies, chances are that if the individual has ever been on television or in a movie, they will have an IMDb page. Many PR agencies and reps also create IMDb profiles for their clients and will list their information in the contact section.

When it comes to gaining endorsements, the most crucial thing to bear in mind is to not be pushy. Send one initial correspondence followed by one or two follow ups within a few weeks of each other. If someone has not replied, chances are they are not interested. Move on.

ESTABLISHING PROTECTIONS

Throughout the entirety of this book, we have covered how your small business can construct its image, grow its audience and engage with them in a way that mirrors that of a large corporation. While this is great, it is also disadvantageous.

Your business will now be more visible. You'll have earned new spectators. But not all of these newfound spectators will be fans or have the best intentions for your business. Now, more than ever, you'll need to be prepared to protect your brand. In this concluding section, I'll guide you through taking all the necessary precautions to do just that.

1. Protecting Your Data

Without question, most things are now done on the computer. Large companies spend millions every year to safeguard and store their data. From data security to backup, companies like Facebook and Google also run massive server farms using large teams of IT staff. They employ enterprise-level security standards to protect their users' data. While your small business might not have a setup that impressive, to move your small business forward in the digital era, it is crucial that you conduct routine data protection measures. These might include: regularly backing up your files and implementing the best security resources available to you. When it comes to backing up your company data, cloud storage sites like Dropbox and Google Cloud are your best friends. Your data is backed up automatically and is stored on high-level data infrastructures. These are the same infrastructures used by companies like Twitter, the Broad Institute, Expedia and Spotify. These services will ensure that you have a Plan B if your computers or network becomes corrupt or gets hacked.

As our reliance on technology grows, hackers too are on the rise. Most often, they target small businesses because they know they don't have the resources to put towards cybersecurity like their large counterparts. To counter this, you should train your employees on necessary protective measures such as using appropriate security software, firewalls, creating strong passwords, and using two-step verification when logging into company systems.

Cybersecurity tools, like Norton Small Business along with Bitdefender's GravityZone Business Security, can provide small businesses with a version of the same tools available to the more prominent players. These include vulnerability assessments and network attack defenses.

2. Protecting Against Lawsuits

Even if you are sure that you would win a lawsuit, they are so costly and time-consuming that avoiding them is the best option. This is why we constantly hear stories in the news of large corporations allegedly paying off litigants and settling cases out of court. But chances are, your small business might not have the funds to follow suit.

Ensure that every interaction you do is formally represented. In other words, ensure that every aspect of your business that mingles with others is covered in writing. Have hiring agreements, client agreements, supplier agreements, privacy policies, terms of services, NDAs and contracts. When it comes to written agreements, avoid standardized templates and policy generators. Every business is different and will face legal challenges in various forms. For example, a construction company would most likely face legal threats surrounding safety and individual welfare, while an indie (independent) production studio might face challenges with copyright law and intellectual property. With that said, seek custom legal documents that are drafted with your business in mind. Services like LegalShield (Canada) and LegalZoom (the United States) provide on-demand legal assistance from legal specialists as well as a network of attorneys. You might consider them a pay-as-you-need legal department.

Lastly, in the eyes of the law, separate yourself from your business. If you have not already, ensure your company is registered as a limited liability company (LLC). This provides a divide between you and your company as it relates to both legal and taxation matters.

3. Protecting Your Reputation

It could take you up to five years to build your reputation, but it will only take five minutes to destroy it. And once it is destroyed, you can hardly go back to the previous place you were. Therefore, it is essential to ensure that you are protecting your company's reputation at all costs.

Be cautious of what you put out there.

Whether it is on your company's social media channels or physical mediums, being cautious of what comes out of your company can spare you a great deal in safeguarding your reputation. Be sure to warn employees not to involve themselves in questionable activities.

Be mindful of who you work with.

Be mindful of the companies you work with. Working with a company that has been blacklisted will lower your reputation too. This applies to the employees you are hiring. Hiring nefarious people will make you look like one yourself.

Be vigilant with what's already out there.

Perhaps the only thing worse than having a bad reputation is not knowing you have one.

Earlier, I mentioned using Google Trends to keep an eye on your market. But what about your reputation? Services like Reputation X and Brand Yourself allow small businesses to monitor the web for negative content related to them. Both companies can also reconstruct a business's reputation that has already been tarnished. They can also produce positive content such as blog articles, press releases and social media posts in an attempt to outrank malicious content about your brand.

CONCLUSION

Since you have made it here, you should now have a reliable map to structuring your small business to look like a large corporation. *Congratulations!*

You will now be ready to command the attention of your audience, increase sales, connect with new business partners, and begin the journey of establishing your company as a market-leader.

Your business should now have:

- A reliable foundation that features a memorable logo, a professional company website, and marketing copy written for your target audience.

- A highly effective structure designed to influence perception. This will include operational departments, communication channels, a robust social presence, and the ability to operate 24/7.

- A toolkit to maintain relevance in your market by utilizing market research, the media, and public figure endorsements.

- Resources to protect and safeguard your company's reputation moving forward.

In closing, I hope you had as great an experience reading **The Marketing Fallacy** as I did writing it. May it be a staple in your business books library, one you can refer to as you continue to grow and expand your small business. I wish you all success as you push forward in this challenging yet rewarding field of entrepreneurship.

ACKNOWLEDGEMENTS

I have many people with whom I am thankful for. They include my family, relatives, business partners, friends and supporters. Thank you all for believing in me and helping me create a book that is designed to support a sector of society that is highly valuable yet often overlooked: small business owners.

Thanks to all of you, I have been issued a platform to share my knowledge and experience. For that, I will be forever grateful.

ABOUT THE AUTHOR

Joshua Littlejohn is an entrepreneur, marketer and founder. In January of 2017, he launched Norgress, a digital media and information technology company where he currently serves as the chief executive officer.

In his role, Joshua is responsible for helping companies achieve their strategic goals, increase revenue, and build customer relations through marketing, client support, information technology and business services. Joshua is also the founder of Get Ready World, a social initiative dedicated to supporting individuals and groups that effect change and influence their world using business, art and culture. Get Ready World also provides resources that encourage people to get involved, be creative and advance the morals and values that contribute to building a more prosperous, safe and open society for all.

Born in Kingston, Jamaica, Joshua is a graduate of the Northern Alberta Institute of Technology (NAIT), where he studied Marketing.

ABOUT THE FONT

This book was published in Avenir Next LT Pro, a contemporary font developed by Adrian Frutiger in collaboration with Akira Kobayashi. The font is issued by the Monotype Corporation and gained much praise after its 2004 release. The word "Avenir" is French for "future." Avenir Next LT Pro is considered one of the best contemporary fonts for print media.

THANK YOU FOR READING

THE MARKETING FALLACY

YOUR AUDIOBOOK IS WAITING FOR YOU

Download your audiobook and listen to it for FREE!

with a 30-day Free Trial to **Audible.com**

If you do not have an Audible or Amazon.com account, you will need to establish an account with Amazon.com to use the service. The payment methods on file with your Amazon.com account will be used for your Audible account. Audible is an affiliate of AmazonServices.com